M000297424

Comstock Park, MI
49321

UNDERSTANDING THE CHAMBON

UNDERSTANDING
THE CHAMBON

ELIZABETH   LAUNDER, MSc
AND
HILARY   LEGARD

J. A. ALLEN
LONDON

British Library Cataloguing in Publication Data
Launder, Elizabeth
1. Horses—Training
I. Title   II. Legard, Hilary
636.1'083   SF287

ISBN 0-85131-439-2

First published 1988
Reprinted 1989

© Elizabeth Launder and Hilary Legard 1988

Illustrations by Christine Bousfield

Published in Great Britain by
J. A. Allen & Company Limited,
1, Lower Grosvenor Place, Buckingham Palace Road,
London, SW1W 0EL

All rights reserved. No part of this book may be reproduced, stored in a
retrieval system, or transmitted, in any form or by any means,
electronic, mechanical, photocopying, recording or otherwise, without
prior permission, in writing, from the publishers

Book production Bill Ireson

Printed and bound in Great Britain by
WBC Bristol & Maesteg

CONTENTS

LIST OF ILLUSTRATIONS

List of Illustrations

INTRODUCTION

The mention of 'schooling' reins or devices in the context of training horses and ponies can be received in a number of ways. To purists or academics these 'contraptions' are considered unnecessary, perhaps harmful or completely useless. On the other hand there are riders reluctant to leave the stableyard without some kind cf 'schooling' device in place; or trainers who habitually use them when schooling or reschooling horses.

Whatever your persuasion, the fact is these devices are widely, and invariably badly used, often causing the horse a great deal of stress and discomfort, and in extreme cases physical and possibly mental damage. The effects of schooling devices on the horse needs to be understood before deciding to use them, and it should be appreciated that in experienced hands they can be helpful. However, wrongly employed they can be abusive to the horse.

Do not take our word for this. Look around and see the many horses or ponies forced to adopt their 'collected poses' largely by the insensitive use of schooling equipment, such as side-reins or draw-reins.

Elizabeth Launder and I decided that guidelines for using some of the more popular schooling devices could help the user to avoid causing their horses unnecessary stress and to promote a greater understanding of, and a more considered approach to, the use of schooling devices.

HJL

ACKNOWLEDGEMENTS

The authors would like to thank Christine Bousfield for her work on the line illustrations; Charles Harris, F.B.H.S., F.A.B.R.S., for his invaluable support; and Kit Houghton and *Horse & Rider* magazine for the photographs they supplied.

Plate 1
Horse equipped for lunging with the Chambon fitted

I

THE CHAMBON

The Chambon is an item of specialised training equipment designed by, and named after, a French cavalry officer who was based at the French Army Equestrian School at Saumur in the early 1900s. Whilst the Chambon achieved considerable popularity on the Continent, particularly in France and Italy, it has not been so widely used in other parts of the world.

The equipment was devised specifically for use whilst lunging the horse, and is used primarily during the schooling of horses who, for a variety of reasons, have not or cannot achieve the 'correct outline' necessary in order to move forward in a balanced, obedient and active manner. Horses with good conformation, who have received the basic schooling necessary in order to achieve the correct novice outline seldom require work with the Chambon; neither should it be necessary when reschooling a horse if adequate time is made available for this process.

The action of the Chambon, if it is used as it was intended to be used, can assist the process of producing a supple, well co-ordinated horse working with the necessary correct outline needed for efficient locomotion, but, the Chambon should be considered as a 'means to an end' *not* the means in itself.

The correct outline is generally successfully developed

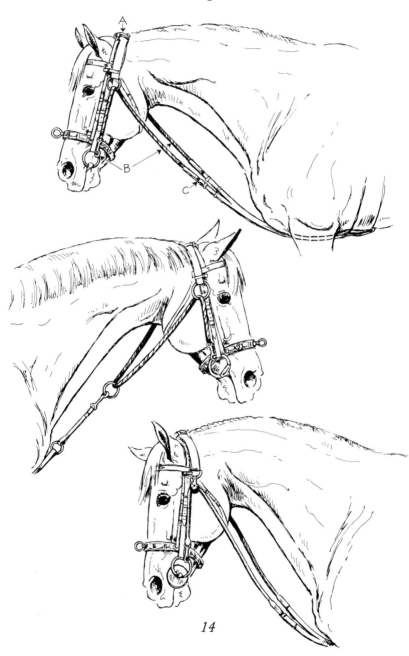

14

without the use of the Chambon. However, if the Chambon is used (Plate 1) it needs to be used considerately.

It is *vital* for the trainer to be able to lunge a horse correctly and effectively *before* attempting to lunge him with the Chambon fitted.

The Chambon (Figure 1) is used in conjunction with a correctly fitted bridle — without a noseband — and eggbutt or loose ring jointed snaffle; with the optional use of rubber discs, a lunging cavesson, and appropriate lunging equipment.

Figure 1 *(opposite)*
Three examples of the Chambon, which are made up of:
  (A) The headpiece;
  (B) two adjustable lengths of corded rope or rolled leather, approximately 1.35 m (4.42 ft) long, with a snaphook at one end, and a strap which buckles onto . . .
  (C) an adjustable leather strap, approximately 1 m (3.28 ft) long, which passes between the horse's front legs and attaches to a roller

II

CORRECT OUTLINES

Efficient locomotion can only be achieved if the horse has been encouraged to work in an outline which allows for the development of the appropriate musculature necessary before he can become a well-balanced active riding or driving horse.

The outline can be classified as follows:

Novice (Plate 2): young horses in their first six months of training and/or racing.

Intermediate (Plate 3): horses engaged in riding, hunting, eventing and showjumping.

Advanced (Plate 4): horses which have progressed to advanced dressage and showjumping.

The outline (Figures 2 and 3) should develop progressively throughout training, but for general riding purposes an intermediate outline is sufficient.

Plate 2
A Novice outline

Plate 3
An Intermediate outline   *18*

Plate 4
An Advanced outline

Figure 2
The correct outline

Figure 3 *(opposite)*
The correct and incorrect outline: *(top)* the correct outline for (A) Novice, (B) Intermediate, (C) Advanced horse; *(bottom)* incorrect outlines

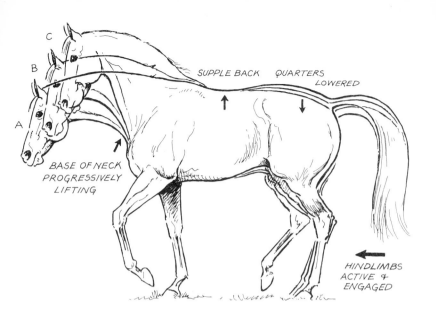

SUPPLE BACK   QUARTERS LOWERED

BASE OF NECK PROGRESSIVELY LIFTING

HINDLIMBS ACTIVE & ENGAGED

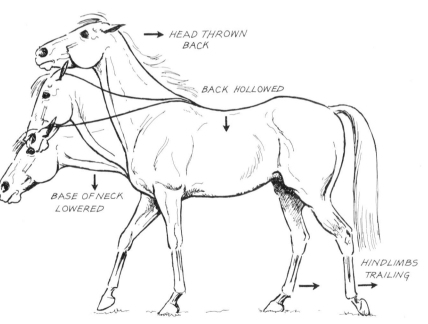

HEAD THROWN BACK

BACK HOLLOWED

BASE OF NECK LOWERED

HINDLIMBS TRAILING

In order to fully appreciate the significance of the horse developing the correct Novice outline, through all gaits, a basic understanding of the skeletal and muscular make-up of the horse is essential.

The horse's conformation is dictated by it's skeletal make-up. The way the skeleton is put together in terms of angulation of the joints, the lengths of the bones of the limbs and the attachment of the limbs to the spine significantly influences the efficiency of the horse's movements.

The horse's skeleton (Figure 4) is made up of approximately 205 bones:

head and skeleton	34
spine and vertebral column	91
forelimbs	40
hindlimbs	40

The spine, which houses the all-important spinal cord, is probably the most fundamental unit of the mammalian skeleton. It links arms and legs, forehand and hindquarters, thereby allowing movement to occur. In the horse, it is also the support from which the heavy internal organs are suspended.

The spine of the horse must have some mobility in order that the animal can lie down, get up, turn around, graze, look up, and so on. Yet it also needs enough rigidity to support the very heavy body and to provide a rigid structure which can accept and transmit the powerful force generated by the hindquarters during locomotion.

To provide both flexibility and rigidity, the spine is made up of:

rigid elements — the vertebrae themselves, and
flexible elements — the ligaments, intervertebral discs and joints between the vertebrae

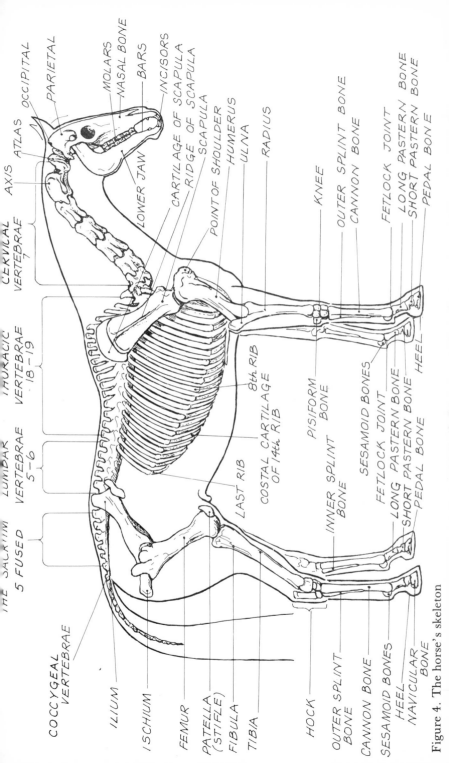

Figure 4. The horse's skeleton

The disc between each vertebrae is a pad of connective tissue which separates the vertebrae, and absorbs concussion. The intervertebral joints and ligaments holding the vertebrae together also enable movement between the vertebrae.

Stability is provided by the muscles of the neck and back which, particularly at speed, contract to hold the back rigid, giving the hindlegs a stable structure against which to push.

The spine is made up of 54 bones:

> 7 cervical or neck vertebrae (C1-7)
> 18 thoracic or dorsal vertebrae (T1-T18/19)
> 6 lumbar vertebrae (L1-L5/6)
> 5 sacral vertebrae fused
> 18 coccygeal vertebrae

All these vertebrae consist of three basic components: the body, arch and processes. The latter are spinous (projecting vertically) and transverse (projecting laterally).

Cervical Vertebrae
The first two neck bones, the atlas and axis, differ structurally from the other vertebrae and from each other. Their vertebral canal, which houses the spinal cord, is of greater diameter — a precaution against damage to the nerve in an area where there is a great deal of movement.

The atlas is simply a ring of bone with a large plate of bone — the wing — on either side. You feel this at the top of the neck just behind the ears. The plate gives a large area of attachment for important neck muscles and ligaments.

The axis has a tooth-like projection — the odontoid process — which extends into the ring of the atlas and so joins the two together. The spinous process of the axis is very large, also providing an area for attachment of the neck muscles and ligaments, namely the ligamentum nuchae.

Ligamentum Nuchae

This ligament is like an elastic cable attached to all neck vertebrae (Figure 5), running over the highest dorsal spines of the wither, and joining with the supraspinous ligament which extends along the back to the sacrum, so joining the tops of the spinous processes of the cervical, thoracic and lumbar vertebrae.

Together, these ligaments act as a kind of hawser: when the poll of the animal stretches forward and down, the back is pulled up. The ligamentum nuchae, which acts as an elastic cable, also supports the head and neck, allowing them to be raised and lowered by the muscles of the neck.

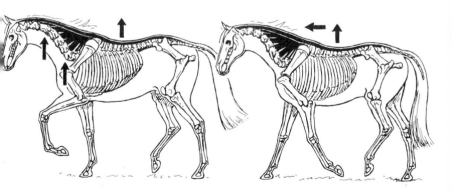

Figure 5
The ligamentum nuchae

Thoracic Vertebrae

Each thoracic vertebrae carries a pair of ribs. The bony projections making up the spinous processes are short in the cervical vertebrae, but those of the first six thoracic bones gradually increase to 15 cm (6 in) to 20 cm (8 in) in length.

The highest is at T4, under which the forelegs are positioned — or should be! They then gradually diminish in size towards the rear. This increase in length gives rise to a curved ridge, the wither, which is made up of vertebrae T3 – T10. The first seven thoracic vertebrae are partly hidden behind the shoulder blade or scapula. The remainder, which can be felt behind the wither, make up the saddle region. It is these bones which suffer most from pinching saddles, rollers, or a heavy rider. They can be found to have arthritis as well as being the site for intercession (rubbing one against the other).

Lumbar Vertebrae

There may be five or six of these, depending upon the origin of the animal. Eastern breeds, namely Arab, tend to have five lumbar vertebrae, in which case they will have an extra thoracic vertebra. The dorsal processes of these vertebrae, up to T15, point backward, but the dorsal processes of T15 – T18 and the lumbar vertebrae, face forwards.

The transverse processes project at right angles and are extremely large — 7.5 cm (3 in) to 10.2 cm (4 in) long and 2.5 cm (1 in) wide. They provide attachment for the powerful muscles of the loin and quarter. The bodies of these vertebrae generally fuse later on in life, but sometimes as early as at two or three years. There is no problem if this occurs equally on both sides, but, if it doesn't it may cause pain or crookedness resulting in impaired performance, until such time as the opposite side has fused.

The Sacrum
Consists of five bones which are fused together and make a solid mass at the point where the pelvis and the spine are joined. This area makes up the croup and is very important as it receives the thrust from the hindlegs.

Coccygeal Vertebrae
There are 18 of these. They lose their articular processes and the nerve canal after about the third, and the end tail bones are just rods of bone united by discs of cartilage.

Horses are thought to have relatively inflexible backs, but the exact degree of movement of each part of the spine is currently under debate. The joint between the occipital bone of the skull and atlas, which makes up the poll, allows nodding, flexion and extension of the head on the neck. This movement is of importance in gaining flexion of the poll. The joint between the atlas and axis enables rotation of the head on the neck with the remaining five neck vertebrae, allowing a considerable amount of sideways or lateral bend, flexion and extension. All movements are important when training the horse.

Backward traction of the reins serves to depress the vertebrae at the base of the neck, raising and pulling back the head (Figure 6). This movement slackens the important ligaments of the neck and back, allowing the spine to hollow, and causing the hindlegs to be pushed out behind so that they find it difficult to flex under the body. The ligaments of the neck and back

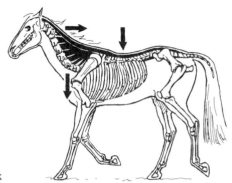

Figure 6
Ligamentum nuchae slack

must be strengthened by training in order to help hold the back up to allow for the correct flexion of the hindlegs.

The head or poll needs to be level with the wither, the head at approximately 45 degrees to the ground for maximum tension to be exerted on these ligaments. If over flexion of the neck and poll occurs, these ligaments will not be held at maximum tension.

If backward traction is exerted on a single rein, then the neck is laterally bent, pushing the base of the neck to the opposite side, bringing the head back on itself, impeding the forward movement of the shoulder on that side.

The skeleton is held together, and given form, by ligaments, tendons and muscles; the latter totalling 540 being divided into involuntary and voluntary muscles. The involuntary muscles make-up the walls of organs: i.e., heart, alimentary canal, blood vessels, bowel and bladder; the voluntary muscles, responsible for locomotion, are divided into superficial and deep muscles. The superficial muscles constitute the outer layers and the deep muscles actually hold the framework together and generate movement (Figures 7 and 8).

Correct Outlines

The Stationary Horse

Gravity acting on the heavy abdominal contents tends to pull the back down, making it hollow. In order that the horse can resist this pull and hollowing, it needs ligaments and muscles.

The ligaments pull the back up and backwards. The upward pull resists the effect of gravity and the backward pull pushes the vertebrae together against the pelvis. This stiffens the vertebral column, making it more rigid to receive the push from the hindquarters. Similarly, when the forelimbs move, muscles are needed to pull the back upwards and forwards.

Canter and Gallop

The head and neck downswing at these gaits is an essential movement: it assists in pulling the back up and away from the ground and aids the forward movement of the animal. This is why it is essential that the head and neck are free for jumping and galloping. The trapezius, longissimus dorsi, spinalis dorsi muscles and ligamentum nuchae are all involved here. Obviously this downswing is affected if the horse holds his head too high and if the reins are too short.

At the slower gaits, the head and neck downswing is not considered to be an important part of forward movement.

Forelimb Locomotion

This is achieved by a number of muscles. Initially, the foot leaves the ground by being lifted by a contraction of the trapezius and rhomboideus muscles. These act most efficiently when the neck is arched correctly. If the head and neck are held too low, or the head too high or overbent, then the trapezius is limited in its action.

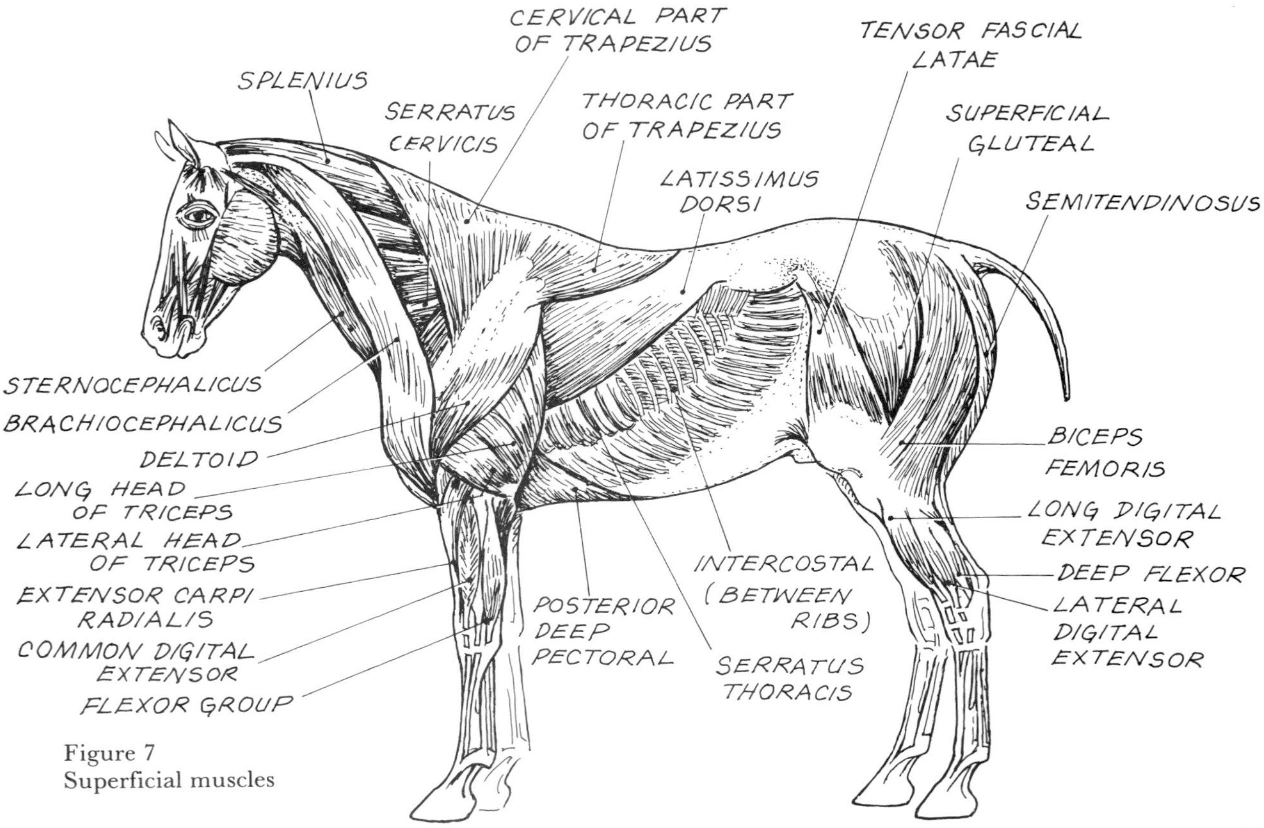

Figure 7
Superficial muscles

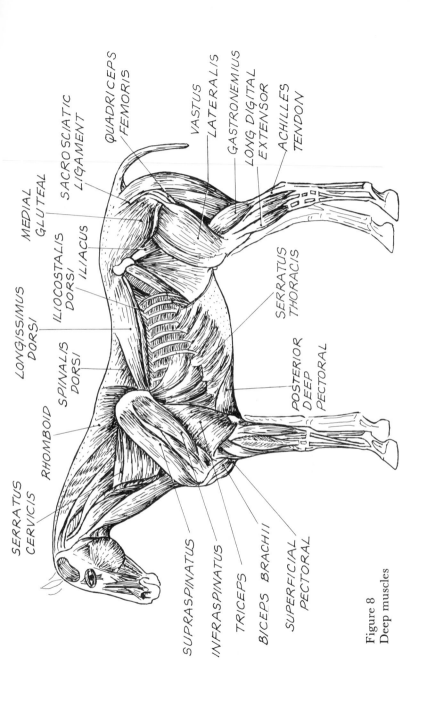

Figure 8
Deep muscles

The brachiocephalic muscle — which runs from the humerus to the head — pulls the leg forward. This muscle works most efficiently when the neck is fully extended. If the head is held too high, with the poll being forced back, the brachiocephalic will pull the limb up as well as forward — hence the knee action of a ewe-necked horse. This emphasises the need for the horse to work parallel to the ground in order to develop correct locomotion.

The trunk of the horse lies in a sling made by the serratus muscles; these are composed of two parts — the cervicis or neck/head part and the thoracis or chest part. The brachiocephalic muscle pulls the leg forward while the serratus thoracis contracts, pulling back and down on the shoulder blade. At the same time, serratus cervicis relaxes. This is known as reciprocal muscle action: as one muscle contracts, its opposing member must relax. This action helps to keep muscle activity smooth, controlled and co-ordinated, preventing jerky, irregular movement.

As the leg swings forward, it bends at the knee. The longer the leg of the horse, the more muscular effort needed to bend and swing the leg forward. This explains the conformational requirement for long forearms and short cannons, and for the leg to be short compared to the body.

The flexion of the horse's leg is followed by extension before impact with the ground. This is brought about by a number of muscles, and specifically the extensor carpi radialis.

Once the leg is fully stretched, the serratus cervicis contracts while the serratus thoracis relaxes. The latissimus dorsi (which lies under the saddle) contracts and the brachiocephalic relaxes, drawing the leg down and back so that the foot hits the ground. As the foot impacts with the ground, the foreleg receives the body weight and the leg must be locked at the knee and elbow so that it can both support the body weight and the appropriate forelimb muscles which assist in moving the horse forward. The body weight coming onto the limb forces the fetlock and coffin joints to flex. Gravity at this point forces the leg back and down. The biceps and serratus cervicis muscles keep the limb straight and the elbow is held extended (locked) by the triceps muscle.

The forward movement of the limb is achieved by the serratus cervicis, the triceps and the deep pectoral muscles; the latter pull the body forward and the leg back. (These muscles become over-developed in horses that pull themselves along with the forelegs.)

Before the foreleg clears the ground, the deep flexor muscles contract, pulling on the hoof, lifting the limb up and forward. When the fore or hindlimb is on the ground supporting the body weight, the back must be prevented from hollowing. This is necessary to provide a rigid structure against which the limbs can push.

In the case of the forehand, the spinalis dorsi muscle contracts to lift the vertebrae and hold the back rigid. When the hindquarters tuck under before hindleg impact, the longissimus dorsi acts to lift the thoracic lumbar spine and hold it rigid. These muscles are inhibited if the horse holds his head and neck high, his back hollow or if he has a very flat croup.

Hindleg Locomotion
The primary function of the forelegs is to support weight, absorb shock and lift the animal from the ground for the flight phase of the stride (the secondary

function is to assist in moving the horse forward), the rear legs provide the main propulsion.

The hindlegs, unlike the forelegs, are attached to the rest of the body by a bony union at the sacrum. Before the leg can move forward, the hip, hock and stifle joint must all flex; this enables the limb to be pulled forward with the least muscular effort.

In walk and trot, one hindleg comes forward (protracts) whilst the other goes backwards (retracts); there is no flexion at the croup. At canter and gallop, both legs protract and retract together, although one is slightly ahead of the other. The lumbasacral joint flexes during protraction and extends during retraction.

The limb is brought forward by contraction of a number of muscles including the superficial gluteal muscle and the tensor fascia latae. At the same time the illiopsoas muscle and the quadratus lumborum hold the spine steady and flex the spine or the hip joint, lifting the leg from the ground.

The stifle is flexed by a portion of the biceps femoris muscle and the hock automatically flexes as a result of an arrangement of muscles on the back and front of the tibia. After the forward phase, the limb swings back and straightens in preparation for impact. This retraction of the limb is brought about by many muscles working together, but mainly by the gluteus medius which is attached at one end to the sacrum and at the other to the femur (thigh bone).

Contraction of the biceps femoris muscle assists the gluteus in this backwards swing, whilst the quadriceps femoris extends the stifle, causing the hock to extend and the fetlock to dorisflex.

In canter and gallop, hindlimb action is assisted by the downswing of the head and neck. As the hindleg

Figure 9
An incorrect outline inhibits efficient movement

drives against the ground, pushing the horse forward, the hip joint extends, the stifle flexes and the hock joint extends, allowing the pastern to lift.

When training and riding a horse it is important to promote correct muscular development and to prevent imbalance. The correct integration of musculature and skeleton is therefore essential for efficient movement to take place (Figure 9).

III

WHEN TO USE THE CHAMBON

The Chambon was designed to assist in achieving the correct novice outline of the horse whilst he is on the lunge and therefore unhindered by the weight of the rider.

Figure 10
The effect of weight on a physically underdeveloped horse. Gravity, the abdominal contents and the rider's weight all contribute to hollowing the horse's back

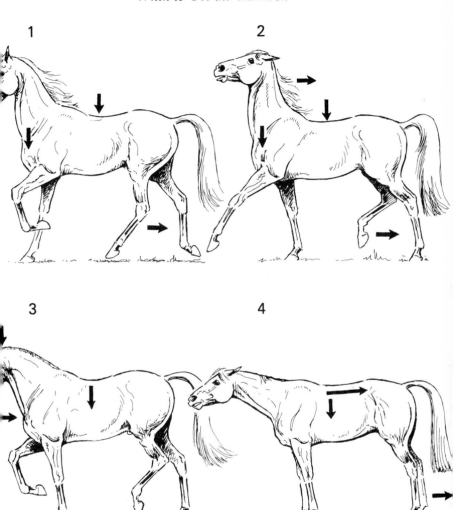

Figure 11
Carriage of the horse. A hollow back with: (1) ewe neck; (2) raised
head; (3) neck overbent; (4) excessive rigidity

1   2

Figure 12 *(this page and opposite)*
Tracking-up: (1) the horse not tracking-up, hindfeet being placed
behind the prints of the forefeet; (2) just tracking-up, the hindfeet just
being placed over the prints of the forefeet; (3) some over-track, hindfeet just past the prints of the forefeet; (4) significant over-track, the
hindfeet being placed 2/4 footfalls past the prints of the forefeet — an
indication of efficient locomotion

It is not advisable to begin systematic lunging — with
or without the Chambon, before a horse is three years
and over and sufficiently physically mature.

If the horse is ridden with the Chambon fitted his
balance can be affected as the Chambon impedes the full
use of his head and neck, which he may need to
maintain balance with the additional weight of the rider
on his back (Figure 10). Also, initially, the rider's weight
can inhibit the development of those major muscles of
the back required for mechanically efficient movement.

In an older horse where problems have arisen due to
incorrect schooling or riding a reluctance to assume a

3   4

correct outline has often both physical and mental causes, and these need to be considered before re-training begins.

In the case of young horses with certain physical shortcomings the aim of schooling with the Chambon is to promote their correct physical development; to encourage them to co-operate both mentally and physically, thus developing suppleness, and thereby averting problems due to excessive tension such as rigidity of the back. As a result of this preparation the horse is helped to assume more easily the required outline at a more advanced stage in his training.

The Chambon can be useful (Figure 11) if the horse carries himself with:

hollow back and raised neck (ewe neck)
hollow back with raised head (star gazer)
hollow back and neck overbent, with the head
  behind the vertical
excessive rigidity of the back

Horses assuming any of the above outlines will show a reduced length and height of stride and an inability to track-up (Figure 12) over-tracking being limited through restricted, and therefore inadequate, use of the back and hindquarters. A high head carriage promotes a short, choppy action in front with restricted use of the shoulders. The overbent horse, with his head behind the vertical, will show a reduced length of stride in front, with subsequent trailing of the hindquarters.

The Chambon can also be helpful with conformational shortcomings, for example, ewe or swan necks which can result in outlines as described above.

Before using the Chambon it is necessary to consider *why* the horse has developed an incorrect way of moving.

IV

INCORRECT MOVEMENT IN HORSES

There are a number of common possible causes of incorrect movement in horses. Some of these are considered below.

Tack
Any item of tack wrongly fitted, can cause discomfort in the horse resulting in evasive behaviour. Evasions may be caused by:

1. Bits which are too thick for the horse's jaws, (Figure 13), preventing him closing his mouth and resulting in dryness and discomfort.
2. Bits which are too severe, too big, too small, or too narrow.
3. Browbands which are too small causing the headpiece to rub or pinch the ears.
4. The saddle pinching the spine, producing inflammation and soreness, or the saddle moving excessively on the back causing friction and pain to the back muscles.

Incorrect Schooling
If the horse is not schooled properly then the chances of producing an incorrect outline are increased.

Figure 13
Too large a bit for the horse's mouth

Figure 14
Forcing an outline

Some examples of incorrect schooling will include:

1. The inadequate development of the horse's musculature before carrying the weight of a rider.
2. Forcing an outline too early in the horse's training through misuse of side-reins, draw-reins and other schooling equipment (Figure 14).
3. A schooling programme not planned to take into account the individual horse's ability and conformation i.e., a long, weak back, very straight hindleg, neck short and thick.

Physical Impediments or Disease
Incorrect movement and/or disobedience can have a physiological basis, for example:

1. Wolf teeth, or the development of sharp edges on molars as a result of undershot, overshot, shear or wave-formed jaws causing discomfort in the mouth; a soft roof of the mouth creating mouthing difficulties.
2. The presence of the navicular syndrome, laminitis or other foot conditions, such as pedal ostitis, sidebone, ringbone, bruised soles and heels.
3. An incorrect pastern/foot axis. (2 and 3 cause the horse to attempt to limit the weight on his forefeet, usually by raising his head or neck.) (Figure 15).
4. Clinical conditions of the back.
5. Sore backs as a result of bumping riders and badly fitting saddles or harness.
6. Problems in the hindlegs: sacroiliac strain, stifle problems, bone spavins, sub-chondral bone cysts.

Figure 15
Alleviating weight on the forefeet

If you are in the *slightest* doubt as to whether there may be some clinical reason why your horse has developed his present way of moving, seek appropriate expert advice: i.e., veterinary or remedial advice.

V

FITTING THE CHAMBON CORRECTLY

On young horses, or those unfamiliar with the Chambon, the equipment should be fitted so that an effect is only felt when the head is carried excessively high. As the horse becomes accustomed to the equipment it should be gradually shortened so that it takes effect only when the horse moves his head and neck outside the specified outline. The length of the Chambon is altered by either making the leather strap between the horse's front legs (Figure 16) shorter or longer, or similarly by adjusting the attachments to the bit. The Chambon is being activated if these attachments are tight when the horse's nose and hip are on approximately the same horizontal level (Figure 17).

(It is not advisable to lead a horse with the Chambon's bit attachments fitted — should he get his head down it is possible for him to catch his feet in the ropes — they should be attached on reaching the schooling area.)

How the Chambon Works
The Chambon comes into effect only when the horse lifts his head and neck above the parallel position necessary for efficient movement at a Novice level. Raising the head increases the tension on the attachments to the bit, thereby moving the bit up into the horse's mouth, placing pressure either on the corners or the roof of the

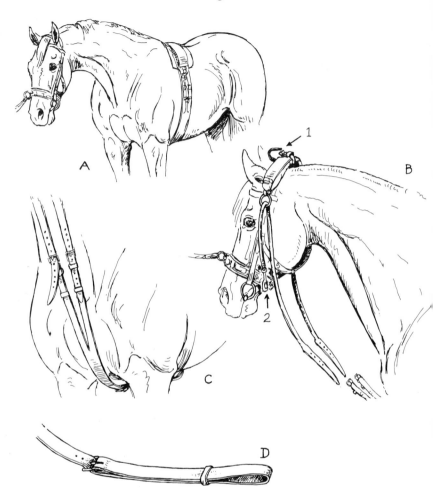

Figure 16
Fitting the Chambon: (A) horse equipped for lunging with a roller and pad, and a snaffle bridle without the noseband, lunging cavesson; (B) the Chambon headpiece is attached to the headpiece of the bridle by the leather strap (1) and the snap hooks (2) clip onto the rings of the bit; (C) and (D) these straps alter the length of the Chambon

46

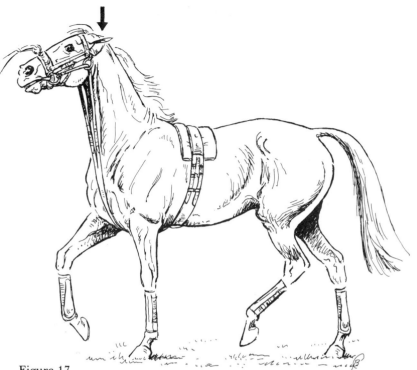

Figure 17
The Chambon being activated

mouth depending upon the position of his head and neck
(Figure 18).

Simultaneous pressure will be applied to the poll from
the Chambon's headpiece which is fastened to that of the
bridle and cavesson. The Chambon inhibits upward
movements of the horse's head and neck, which he is
otherwise free to move sideways, forwards and
downwards. The Chambon does not apply any
backward pressure on the mouth. The horse's reaction
to the Chambon effect should be to lower his head,
thereby allowing the snaffle to slip back into its original
position, a movement which encourages the horse to
salivate and mouth the bit.

Plate 5
Horse being lunged whilst equipped with the Chambon. Note the
pleasing outline in walk

Plate 6
A horse with an inverted outline — a suitable candidate for the
Chambon

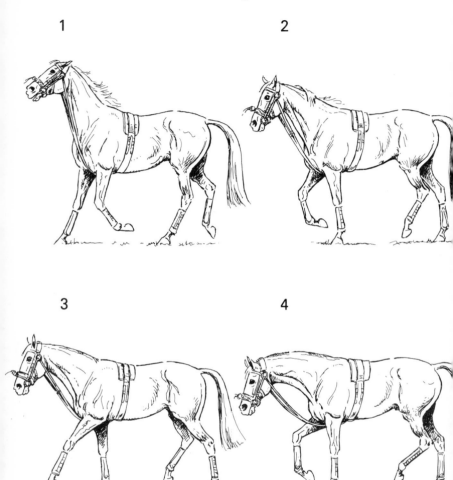

Figure 18

The Chambon effect: (1) bit being raised in the horse's mouth, simultaneous pressure is brought to bear on the poll; (2) the horse responding by a slight lowering of the head; (3) a further response, producing a significant lowering of the head and neck; (4) the 'Chambon effect', resulting in the correct Novice outline

VI

USING THE CHAMBON

The objectives of lunging, with or without the
Chambon, are to improve the posture, balance,
suppleness and gaits of the horse. The equipment for
lunging will include:

> lunge rein, approximately 10 m (32 ft) long, with a
> leather fastening
> lunge whip of 2.5 m (8 ft) length with a lash of
> sufficient length to make it possible to touch the
> horse's hocks with the end of the lash without the
> trainer having to move forward
> brushing boots on all four legs
> lunging cavesson
> roller and pad

Lunge the horse (Figure 19) from the cavesson on a
circle suitable for the size of the horse: i.e., not smaller
than 20 m (65.5 ft) diameter for 15.2hh upwards and
not smaller than 15 m (49 ft) diameter for horses or
ponies under this.

While lunging the horse do not allow him to fall in or
fall out on the circle (Figure 20). He should move with
his quarters level. The gait and tempo of the horse need
to be chosen carefully. While certain horses intially
benefit from a slower tempo, others may need to be
driven forward strongly (Figure 21) to compel them to

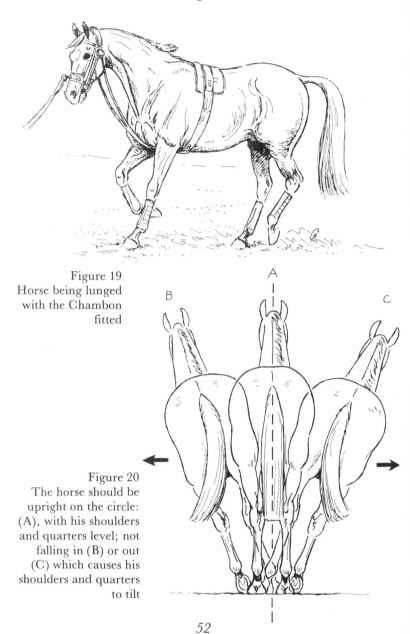

Figure 19
Horse being lunged
with the Chambon
fitted

Figure 20
The horse should be
upright on the circle:
(A), with his shoulders
and quarters level; not
falling in (B) or out
(C) which causes his
shoulders and quarters
to tilt

52

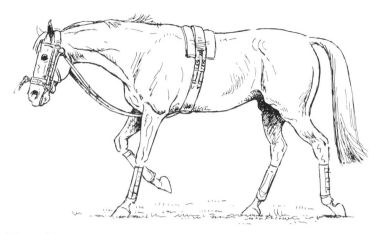

Figure 21
A slack horse with insufficient co-ordination between fore and hindquarters

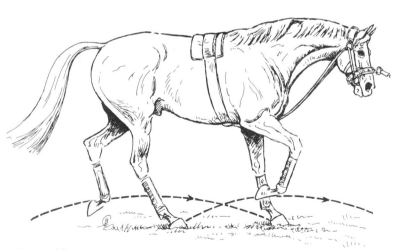

Figure 22
Horse moving correctly on the lunge, with significant over-track

use their head and neck for balance, with the result that they have to stretch their head and neck forward and down (Figure 22) so that their poll is level with their withers, the neck parallel to the ground and the head assuming an angle of approximately 45 degrees to the neck. This position encourages maximum tension on the ligamentum nuchae and dorsal ligaments of the spine causing the vertebrae in the base of the neck to be lifted, and the back to be held with the degree of rigidity necessary in order for the push of the hindleg against the ground to be effectively transferred to the trunk of the horse, hence creating forward movement.

If the horse does not respond initially to the influence of the Chambon it may be necessary to increase the tension on the bit attachments, carefully shortening these, until the horse shows some indication that he understands what is required of him. Ultimately it is up to the trainer's judgement to assess the correct length of the Chambon for each individual horse.

If, after the initial introductory phase, insufficient tension is applied to the bit limited results will be achieved. Once the horse has understood what is required of him then he should continue being worked on the lunge in both directions, at walk, trot and canter.

When used correctly, on appropriate horses, the effect of the Chambon helps to strengthen and develop the muscles of the back, loins and hindquarters (Figures 23 and 24).

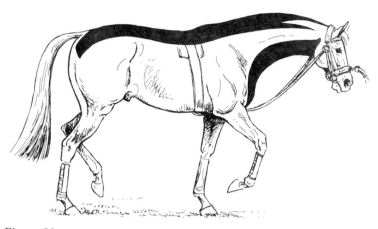

Figure 23
A horse assuming a correct Novice outline will ultimately develop the
appropriate musculature for efficient locomotion

Figure 24
Incorrect outline encourages the over-development of musculature on
the underside of the horse's neck

VII

A SUGGESTED LESSON PLAN

The overall length of any lesson should not exceed 30 minutes. The aim is to develop efficiency of locomotion and posture in both directions: i.e., on the left rein and right rein. This does not necessarily mean equal lunging in both directions. If, for example, the horse resists more to the right, work longer on this side during the first and subsequent lessons. Once equality of function is achieved, work equally both ways, changing direction at frequent intervals. During any lesson the horse should be brought frequently to walk and halt. This provides important rest periods and promotes obedience. The walk should be kept active but unhurried, the strides long, regular and showing good over-track.

The walk periods allow the heart and respiratory rate, raised during trot and canter, to return to near normal.

Adrenalin-release is also promoted through exercise. This hormone triggers the horse's natural over-riding 'fight' and 'flight' mechanism — therefore walk and halt can help restore equilibrium.

When the horse is lunging quietly and is accustomed to the Chambon, any lesson should develop the diagonal and lateral limb syncrony and co-ordination equally. Therefore at least 50 per cent of the lesson should be walk/canter and 50 per cent trot. Varying the gaits and tempo helps to keep the horse mentally alert, as well as assisting his physical development.

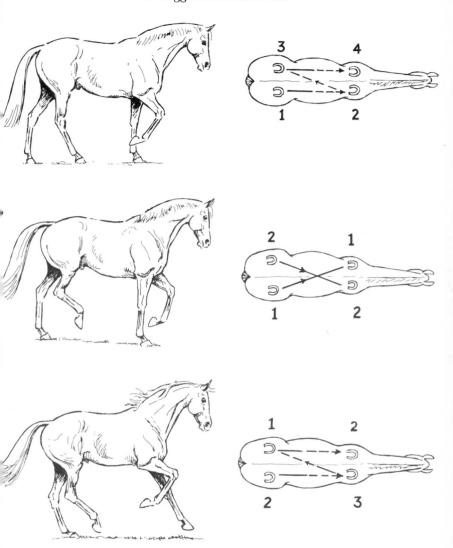

Figure 25
The three gaits: *(top)* walk; *(centre)* trot; *(bottom)* canter

Figure 26 *(this page and opposite)*
A trot sequence

The three gaits (Figure 25) are:

The *walk,* a lateral gait of 4-time, the limbs moving individually: right hind, right fore, left hind, left fore; or left hind, left fore, right hind, right fore.

The *trot,* a diagonal gait of 2-time, the limbs moving in pairs: left hind x right fore, right hind x left fore; or right hind x left fore, left hind x right fore.

The *canter,* a lateral gait of 3-time. The sequence of limbs is: right hind, left hind x right fore, left fore; or left hind, right hind x left fore, right fore.

The trot sequence with diagonal limb syncrony has a marked difference to the walk and canter (Figure 26).

If trot is used excessively the efficiency of the diagonal gait will exceed that of the lateral gaits, making canter

COMPLETE SUSPENSION

and walk difficult to achieve.

The first time the horse gives a response to the Chambon by assuming the correct outline he should be worked for two or three circles in both directions, then finish the lesson for that day. Thereafter, the period of work should be increased in stages of approximately 10 minutes a day, up to 30 minutes.

Once the horse can maintain the correct outline comfortably for 30 minutes, and works with a good rhythm, over-tracking by at least two to three hoofprints, and has muscled-up significantly — which may take up to eight weeks — Chambon work can cease, and a suitable schooling programme may then be followed.

VIII

MISUSE OF THE CHAMBON

It is *important to remember* that using the Chambon is a
'means to an end'. Prolonged, or excessive use, over and
above that which is necessary to consolidate the outline
aimed for, could eventually fix the horse in a long, low
outline, and consequently create difficulties in the
development of a more advanced outline. For example,
it develops pushing power of the hindquarters in a
horizontal plane, and swing of the shoulders without any
elevation of stride.

The length of time the Chambon is used should be
built up gradually to 30 minutes, as initially it will be
tiring for the horse to maintain the outline with the
Chambon fitted. Forcing the horse to hold this position
for any length of time, before he is ready, can cause
over-stress expressing itself in muscle fatigue which
ultimately could lead to loss of co-ordination in the limbs
over-exerting the tendons resulting in lameness.

At times, specifically during re-training, when the
horse has started to move from his inefficient form of
locomotion to a more efficient shape, he may start to
stumble and show some loss of co-ordination. This is
due to the musculature being neither adequately
developed to hold the new form, nor strong enough in
the old form for any kind of co-ordinated movement to
take place. If this happens walk the horse out inhand for

two to three days before continuing the training
programme.

A great deal more can be achieved during schooling if
the trainer is aware that a horse can be over-stressed, in
both mind and body, by too forceful or excessive
training methods.

Readers of this book who wish to be informed about new and forthcoming publications on horses and horsemanship are invited to send their names and addresses to:

J. A. ALLEN & CO. LTD.,
1, Lower Grosvenor Place,
Buckingham Palace Road,
London, SW1W 0EL